How and what do animals learn?

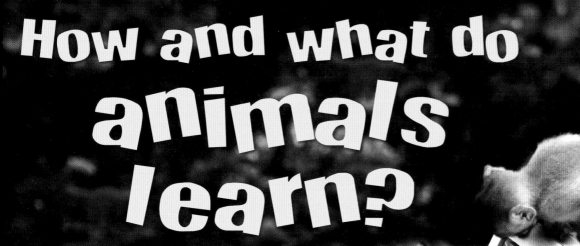

Bobbie Kalman

 Crabtree Publishing Company

www.crabtreebooks.com

All About Animals Close-Up

Dedicated by Bobbie and Peter
For Gabriel Adrian Berti,
Kathy's handsome little prince.
You are adorable, Gabriel!

Author and editor-in-chief
Bobbie Kalman

Publishing plan research and development
Reagan Miller

Editor
Kathy Middleton

Proofreader
Crystal Sikkens

Design
Bobbie Kalman
Katherine Berti
Samantha Crabtree (logo)

Photo research
Bobbie Kalman

Prepress technician
Samara Parent

Print and production coordinator
Margaret Amy Salter

Photographs
Digital Vision: page 19 (top left)
Dreamstime: page 20 (bottom)
Thinkstock: page 8 (bottom left); page 15 (bottom)
Shutterstock: Cover and all other photographs

Library and Archives Canada Cataloguing in Publication

Kalman, Bobbie, author
    How and what do animals learn? / Bobbie Kalman.

(All about animals close-up)
Includes index.
Issued in print and electronic formats.
ISBN 978-0-7787-1462-0 (bound).--ISBN 978-0-7787-1468-2 (pbk.).--
ISBN 978-1-4271-7634-9 (pdf).--ISBN 978-1-4271-7628-8 (html)

        1. Learning in animals--Juvenile literature. 2. Parental behavior
in animals--Juvenile literature. I. Title.

QL785.K34 2015   j591.5'13   C2014-908190-1
                                                         C2014-908191-X

Library of Congress Cataloging-in-Publication Data

Kalman, Bobbie, author.
 How and what do animals learn? / Bobbie Kalman.
    pages cm. -- (All about animals close-up)
 Includes index.
  ISBN 978-0-7787-1462-0 (reinforced library binding : alk. paper) --
 ISBN 978-0-7787-1468-2 (pbk. : alk. paper) --
 ISBN 978-1-4271-7634-9 (electronic pdf : alk. paper) --
 ISBN 978-1-4271-7628-8 (electronic html : alk. paper)
 1. Animal behavior--Juvenile literature. 2. Parental behavior in animals--
Juvenile literature. 3. Animal intelligence--Juvenile literature. 4. Instinct--
Juvenile literature. I. Title. II. Series: Kalman, Bobbie. All about animals
close-up.

  QL751.5.K33635 2015
  591.5--dc23
                                    2014049629

Crabtree Publishing Company

www.crabtreebooks.com   1-800-387-7650

Printed in Canada/042015/BF20150203

Published in Canada
Crabtree Publishing
616 Welland Ave.
St. Catharines, Ontario
L2M 5V6

Published in the United States
Crabtree Publishing
PMB 59051
350 Fifth Avenue, 59th Floor
New York, New York 10118

Published in the United Kingdom
Crabtree Publishing
Maritime House
Basin Road North, Hove
BN41 1WR

Published in Australia
Crabtree Publishing
3 Charles Street
Coburg North
VIC 3058

Contents

How do animals learn?

Animals need to learn important things to keep themselves alive. They learn how to move, find their way, and look for food. They learn how to "talk" to one another. They also learn how to avoid being eaten by **predators**. How do they learn to do these things? People are also animals. How do we learn what we need to keep ourselves alive?

Monkey mothers take care of their babies and teach them the things they need to know to stay alive.

4

How do you learn?

There are many things that you have learned to do since you were born. What other things will you learn as you grow? How will you learn?

5

 # On their own

People and some animals are helpless when they are born and must learn how to do most things from their parents. Some animals, however, are not taught. They know how to survive, or stay alive, on their own. Most reptiles, frogs, and fish leave their babies before or after they hatch, or come out of eggs. The babies know how to stay alive.

After they hatch, chameleons look after themselves.

Mother pythons keep their eggs warm until the eggs hatch. They then leave the babies.

Sea turtle mothers swim a long way back to the beach where they hatched from eggs. They lay many eggs in the sand and then leave. When the baby turtles hatch, they crawl across the beach to the ocean. They know how to crawl and swim. They also know what kind of food they will need to eat and where to find it in the ocean.

This green sea turtle has found sea grasses to eat at the bottom of the ocean.

What do you think?

Many predators feed on baby sea turtles. Why do you think turtle mothers lay so many eggs?

7

Bird parents

Birds also hatch from eggs. Many bird mothers make nests for their eggs, where the chicks, or baby birds, will hatch and grow. Unlike most reptiles, adult birds sit on their eggs to keep them warm until the eggs hatch. One or both parents then take care of the babies. One parent keeps the babies safe from predators, while the other parent looks for food. Birds start flying after they have grown adult feathers.

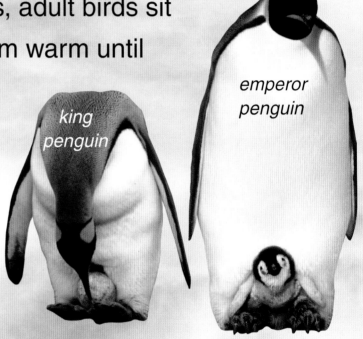

king penguin

emperor penguin

Father king and emperor penguins keep eggs and chicks warm in a pouch that covers their feet.

How and what do they learn?

There are many kinds of birds, but not all can fly. Some birds that cannot fly learn to run or swim. No matter how they move, all chicks need to learn how to find the right kinds of food and how to avoid predators.

Sandhill cranes live in family groups. Both parents look after and teach their chicks.

Hummingbird mothers take care of their chicks until the chicks learn to fly and find their own food.

Penguins cannot fly. They use their wings to swim. Their parents do not teach them how to swim. The chicks learn to do it with other young penguins.

What do you think?

What kinds of lessons do bird parents teach their babies? Why would baby birds not survive without help from their parents?

What do mammals learn?

This female mountain goat is teaching her kids, or babies, to climb a steep mountain safely.

Cats, bears, goats, deer, monkeys, and many other animals are mammals. People are mammals, too. Mammals give birth to live babies. The babies are helpless when they are born. Mammal mothers care for the babies and teach them how to **communicate**, find food, move around in their habitats, and keep safe. Mammal babies could not survive on their own.

This baby monkey is learning how to climb a tree and find food. Its mother is nearby to keep her baby safe.

This fawn, or young deer, will soon learn why it should not go near skunks. What nasty lesson will it learn?

This black bear cub is crying for its mother. Is it afraid it will fall? Baby mammals must learn to communicate to stay alive.

What do you think?

Mammal mothers teach their babies how to keep safe. What are these babies learning? How is what they learn the same or different from what you learn?

Finding food

Different animals eat different kinds of food, and they need to learn how to find it. **Herbivore** mothers teach their babies which plants are good to eat. Carnivores eat other animals, and predators hunt them. Omnivores learn to look for both plants and animals to eat.

Kangaroos are herbivores. This kangaroo joey, or baby, lives in its mother's pouch. It sees the grasses its mother eats and will eat the same foods.

This lion pride, or group, is going hunting. The cubs learn to hunt by watching the adults. Most of the hunting is done by females.

What do you think?

What kinds of foods do you eat? Are you a herbivore, omnivore, or carnivore? Where do you get your food and who makes your meals?

Omnivores eat both plants and meat. Raccoons are omnivores that eat any food they find—even dead animals.

Social animals

Social animals are animals that need to be with other animals and often belong to groups. Many animals hunt together, travel together, and live together. Elephants, dolphins, lions, prairie dogs, monkeys, apes, and wolves are all social animals. People are social animals, too. We need to be with other people.

Female elephants spend their whole lives in family groups called herds. Herds are made up of three pairs of mothers and their babies. Their leader is the oldest female. She leads the herd to food and water.

Bonobos are apes that belong to groups called troops. Being part of a group is very important in how the babies learn. What will this baby learn from her troop?

Dolphins are very social. They live with family and friends in large groups called pods. Dolphins travel and hunt together. They have huge brains and teach their young new ways of hunting. Dolphins also love to have fun!

How they communicate

This girl is chatting with a friend on her tablet. She is waving and saying hello. Is the bear below waving hello, too?

To communicate is to exchange information, ideas, and feelings with others. People talk, write, sing, laugh, and use **body language** to communicate with others. Animals cannot speak, but they do communicate. They use their senses, such as sight, hearing, touch, taste, and smell to send messages to other animals. Some make scary sounds. Others use colors and patterns to attract other animals or scare them away.

These Japanese cranes are doing a dance to show that they are choosing each other as **mates**. It is called a courtship dance.

The bright colors on this poison-arrow frog warn predators that eating this frog can kill them.

neck frill

This lizard opened its neck frill, or flap of skin, to make itself look bigger to a predator.

What do you think?

Do you have a pet? How does it communicate with you? How does it let you know when it is hungry, scared, or wants attention? How do dogs tell you that they want to go for a walk?

Learning to use tools

People used to think that only humans could use tools. Now we know that many animals use tools, too. Several animals use rocks to break open their food. Chimpanzees and some birds use sticks to pull insects out of trees or insect hills to eat them. People have even taught some elephants how to paint!

This talented elephant in Thailand has painted a picture of itself on a shirt.

A mother chimpanzee is teaching her baby how to use a stick to pull ants out of an ant hill. They will then lick the ants off the stick.

This baby squirrel monkey is making a tool from a stick. It is an omnivore that eats fruits, nuts, and insects. How might it use this tool to find insects and get fruit from trees?

What do you think?

Compare the tools used by these animals to some of the tools you use. Which tool is the same as one that you use at school?

Leaf-cutter ants use the leaves they collect to grow their own food.

Super senses!

We have five senses—sight, hearing, smell, taste, and touch. Our senses help us do many things. Many animals have senses that are very different or much stronger than our senses. We need computers and other equipment to do some things that animals can do using just their senses. What super senses do animals have?

Dolphins and some bats use **echolocation**. They create sounds and then use the **echoes** of the sounds to find and identify objects. Echolocation allows animals to see and hear with sound. How do people use sound?

How do they find their way?

Many birds and other animals **migrate**. Monarch butterflies migrate before winter and then fly back home again in spring. They fly from southern Canada, through the United States, all the way to Mexico.

*Monarch butterflies do not learn the flight route to Mexico by using a computer or **GPS**. They have a built-in compass in their brains that points them in the direction they need to travel.*

Our super brains

People cannot do what some animals can do, but we have learned to invent tools to do almost anything. We have huge brains that can learn how to fly planes, create music, do math and science, and speak many languages. Could we someday use our brains to do some of the things animals can do? What hidden animal senses might our brains have? (See the website on page 23.)

This boy's brain shows some of the things we can learn, but our brains can do much more! With a group of classmates, do some research on animal senses and think of some amazing things our brains might do in the future.

Learning more

Books

Kalman, Bobbie. *How do baby animals learn?* (It's fun to learn about baby animals). Crabtree Publishing Company, 2012.

Kalman, Bobbie. *Animal Mothers* (My World). Crabtree Publishing Company, 2011.

Kalman, Bobbie. *What senses do animals have?* (Big Science Ideas). Crabtree Publishing Company, 2009.

Kalman, Bobbie. *How do animals communicate?* (Big Science Ideas). Crabtree Publishing Company, 2009.

Kalman, Bobbie. *Animal Families* (Introducing Living Things). Crabtree Publishing Company, 2008.

Websites

WWF: Five remarkable animal moms
www.worldwildlife.org/stories/five-remarkable-animal-moms

YouTube: Ultimate Animal Moms: Mom's Lessons
www.youtube.com/watch?v=bjEDaqpB8DM

Neuroscience for Kids: Amazing Animal Senses
https://faculty.washington.edu/chudler/amaze.html

Words to know

body language (BOD-ee LANG-gwij) noun A way of communicating using posture, gestures, and facial expressions

communicate (kuh-MYOO-ni-keyt) verb To exchange information, ideas, and feelings with others

echo (EK-oh) noun A repetition of sound

echolocation (ek-oh-loh-KEY-shuh-n) noun An animal's ability to find its way by sending and receiving sounds

GPS (g-p-s) noun Short for Global Positioning System; a system that uses satellites to find the location of places and things

herbivore (HUR-buh-vawr) noun An animal that eats mainly plants

mate (meyt) noun A partner for making babies

migrate (MAHY-greyt) verb To move to another area for better weather, to find food and water, or to have babies

predator (PRED-uh-tawr) noun An animal that hunts other animals for food

A noun is a person, place, or thing.
A verb is an action word that tells you what someone or something does.

Index